PERSPECTIVES

Reflections on continuous
improvement, authenticity
and the power of building
meaningful workplace cultures

KRISTIN **TULL**
LEE ANN **COCHRAN**
THERESE **ZDESAR**

SMART BUSINESS® BOOKS
An Imprint of Smart Business® Network Inc.

Perspectives
COPYRIGHT © 2019 Kristin Tull, Lee Ann Cochran and Therese Zdesar

Published by Smart Business Books
An imprint of Smart Business Network Inc.
835 Sharon Drive, Suite 200
Westlake, OH 44145

Printed in the United States of America
Editor: Dustin S. Klein
Interior Design: April Grasso
Cover Design: Wendy Armon

ISBN: 978-1-945389-50-4
Library of Congress Control Number: 2019907279

CONTENTS

EDITOR'S NOTE

Life is a journey. Some days, the road is smoother than others. Other days, you spend more time avoiding the potholes and obstacles than focusing on either the destination or enjoying the travels. As technology has become ever more embedded in our lives and nearly eliminated the separation between work lives and personal lives, it's never been more important to pull off the road for just a minute and assess the overall journey we've embarked upon.

Where are we headed? How are we getting there? Why are we going? The truth is that what's important to one person may not be as important to another. What motivates one of us may not provide the same spark for somebody else. No matter what separates us, it's what we have in common that matters most: We become our best selves when we strive to be authentic. We are happier and have better relationships when we know our strengths and weaknesses and devote time to self-improvement. And, we thrive best in a positive work environment where people treat each other with respect and care about each other's wellbeing.

On the pages that follow, three dynamic women leaders offer their perspectives on these issues as they explore what matters in people's lives and the impact each one of us can have on every person whose lives we touch.

Kristin Tull explains why it's important to create a sense of purpose through personal development and continuous improvement. Lee Ann Cochran takes you on a journey to understand who you are and how to express your authentic self. And Therese Zdesar offers a glimpse at how powerful a workplace can become when leaders and team members invest time, energy and resources to forge and foster a workplace of caring.

At its core, *Perspectives* is more than just three women's personal and professional experiences. It's a look at how that critical intersection of personal and professional lives in a technology-laden 24/7 society impacts all of us and can either make or break our best selves.

Personal Journey of Development
KRISTIN TULL

Throughout my life, I have adopted a continuous improvement mindset in everything I do—in my work, as a leader, as a family member. I have learned the most from the more difficult things in life and have come to take every setback as a step toward something better.

Not long ago, I delivered a presentation on resilience and the importance of seeing failure as being one step closer to success. In my work with others, I like to help people build on their strengths and improve upon their weaknesses, so they can be better versions of themselves.

Potential customers and clients often ask if people really change. Most people can make changes to be better, but the changes will likely be moderate and implemented over time. If a person has awareness and the motivation to be better, he or she can improve. Much of my career satisfaction has stemmed from helping people be better, happier, and more aligned with what is important to them. We have the ability to impact people in such substantial ways... why not have a positive impact and leave others better than you found them? This has become an important mantra to me both in work and in life, and it guides my personal journey of development. When I help guide others on their own journey of development, it is important to know the outcomes for which they are looking. My goal as a coach might be for somebody to be a better leader, but they need to feel good about that for it to be a success. People aren't going to embrace feedback or suggestions if we don't have a positive interaction, and they really won't be focused on developing unless they work on what matters most to them.

Leading with "I think you should do this," or, "If I were you, I would—" is too directive. People don't want us to tell them what to do. So, why should we? We aren't in their day-to-day business. But if you build the relationship—if people know you have their best interests at heart and if you are adaptable to their style—it becomes a lot easier for them to be open and accept help.

I have been coaching one HR leader for several years, and when we first got started, she was technically capable but admittedly a little lacking on the interpersonal side of things. I spent a good deal of time in the early days listening and validating what she was good at, as well as delicately pointing out what I thought she could do differently. It took some time, but she opened up more and more, and I was able to be a sounding board and someone who could share difficult messages because she knew my one and only goal was to help her be successful. Once we developed trust and a comfort level, she would count on me to tell her what she needed to hear, not what she wanted to hear. It's been a healthy experience for her and she has grown in her career, in large part because of the improvements she has made through our coaching.

Benefits of a Personal Journey of Development

The benefits of coaching stem from whatever the goals are. If you think about what people really want in life, they want to feel valued, be happy, and have some acceptable level of stress. Stress is a constant, but it needs to be balanced and constructive. So, if we identify the right things to work on to reduce stress, the outcome is a better life. If I leave here every day frustrated because my expectations are so crazily high, then I'm not living a good life. I need to figure out a way to get my expectations met so that when I leave, I feel good. The definition of "good" is what matters—did I make a good decision, did I help someone through a difficult situation, did I make progress toward the end goal. These things make me feel valued and accomplished and give me the strength to come back the next day.

The same goes for the people we coach. Although they may want the benefits and to feel better, some people are resistant at first to feedback and coaching. However, over time, many come to see the value. They see the improvement that comes from making changes. Many take a very professional, formal approach to coaching. We don't talk about family or personal issues unless people bring them up themselves but, other times, people will say "I have the same problem at home, or 'my wife would tell you the same thing.'" For these people, they can apply the same changes with their spouse, kids, and friends—as well as in the workplace.

It is not enough, however, to just realize what changes have to be made. A commitment to making changes—or to the process that will help make these changes—is required for coaching to work. People who are fully engaged walk away from a coaching process with a successful model of improvement and a personal development plan. Development is a continuous process, and one that is never finished.

One other important element of a successful development program is time. We hurry through our days without pausing or reflecting on how things are going. It's important to check in every day on what went well and what didn't, what got accomplished and what is still left to do. Many people comment that what they appreciate most about the coaching is spending time on themselves and what matters most to them in their lives, rather than running full speed ahead without much time to think or plan.

In addition to committing to the process and realizing there will always be room for improvement, it is also important to accept credit for what's good. I've seen successful leaders create reflection journals to keep track of their accomplishments and lists of successes on a daily basis; otherwise those are taken for granted.

Often, we tend to focus on and address what's wrong instead of noticing and reacting to what is right. Many people don't realize while this is a journey of development, self-improvement is more than just pointing out what is wrong with yourself and fixing it; it can also be learning to appreciate good qualities and accomplishments and building upon them.

Once someone is ready to proceed with their personal journey of development, we stand ready to help. It is a team effort. We can't force someone to change (nor would we want to), and a personal coach needs to be equally as committed. I am highly driven to help people get to where they want to be, and we can help with defining what success looks like and how best to get there. In my experience, people really can change and, many want to, they just don't know what to do differently. I take a great deal of pride in helping people determine what is important to them, or what they may be doing that is holding them back. Coaching can come in the form of offering tangible suggestions or in asking thought-provoking questions…it all depends on what people need at a given time.

As an example, I have been working with a CEO of a large, global company for several years now, and in year three my value to him is much different than it was in year one. Initially, he was looking for suggestions to successfully transition into his new role along with help reorganizing his leadership team. I also believe that people need to be reminded of their strengths and why they received the promotion they did, as confidence can waiver even for the most seasoned leaders, so I focused on that with him as well. Fast forward to now, we meet on a quarterly schedule and I've been told he most values the questions that I ask that cause him to think about things differently. I also see that he feels stronger and more energized when he leaves our meetings because of the reinforcement I can provide and the candid conversations we have. In high-level roles, these things are highly needed and often hard to come by.

As a coach, I feel valued and satisfied when I can understand what people need and provide it in an honest and constructive way to leave them feeling better than when I found them.

Several years ago, we did some work with Simon Sinek's "Start With Why." Sinek is well known for challenging people to find their "why" or the thing that inspires them on the job and in life. It's more than what you do or how you do it, but why you do what you do that is inspiring. If people understand their "why" and act and lead accordingly, leaders gain followership more easily and everyone goes home at the end of the day feeling more valued and fulfilled. After studying his work, I realized my "why" is to help people live the lives they want to live; it's helping people through their personal journeys of development. I enjoy helping people determine (a) what they want to happen and (b) the best way to get there.

My "why" statement is somewhat vague by design, because what people want can be varied—it can be to work more or to work less, to enter a new relationship or to leave one, to advance and climb the corporate ladder or to excel in one's current position. My best days are the ones where I help people see what they want for themselves and put them on a better path to get there.

Success in a Journey of Personal Development

To succeed in a personal journey of development, self-awareness is key. Self-awareness is knowing and understanding one's own character, emotions, motives and behaviors. Some people are highly self-aware, and they have a good sense of what makes them tick. Others aren't as aware so they may need help from other sources to better understand themselves. Just as there is more than one way to learn new things, there are many ways to develop self-awareness. It can come from self-reflection, input from others or from evaluating past experiences. Self-awareness is different for every person. And from a developmental perspective, it's important to know what you want, what you are good at, and what you want to improve.

Without awareness, people don't know where to focus their efforts. A lot of what we do at PRADCO involves psychological testing. We have a proprietary suite of assessment tools that provide insight into people's motivational drivers, ways to approach work, interpersonal skills, leadership behaviors, and decision-making styles. We measure personality factors and cognitive skills too, but the majority of our focus is on behaviors, because behavior can be changed. A person's intellectual horsepower is largely fixed, but by leveraging different behaviors, deficits can be minimized.

One of our most widely used tools is our Quick View™ Leadership Assessment. It measures 50 behaviors, and our forced choice format points out true strengths, overused strengths, and areas that could be improved. People are often validated when they see how well they do in key areas such as presence, motivating others, and getting results through others. And when scores are low, people have a way to focus their efforts to be better. Many times, people have not been given any direct feedback, or what they have been given isn't particularly actionable. Using assessment data can help people build their confidence and enhance their self-awareness by gathering objective data in a constructive way.

Not every low score is a weakness either. Just because you don't do something doesn't mean it needs to be done, unless there's a purpose for it. If you don't understand a certain concept, learning it won't help you achieve your professional goals unless that concept is necessary for success in your job.

There are three awareness factors on our assessment: self-awareness, which is knowing oneself; interpersonal awareness, which is picking up on cues in others; and then there's organizational awareness, which is understanding group and cultural dynamics.

Self-awareness is people understanding themselves and monitoring their own thoughts and feelings. Being overly self-aware though, can be an overused strength. Being too high can result in overthinking and analyzing too much which can be a distraction. But for the most part, it's a strength because it allows people to get a read on themselves and act intentionally instead of being reactive.

Interpersonal awareness is being a good observer and picking up on cues in others. It's an important skill for people who are in sales and in management because if they are not aware of how other people are receiving them, they could make some missteps without meaning to do so. Interpersonal awareness is often an area of focus when trying to be a better motivator. It's good to be in tune with others to know the best way to influence them. To get better at this, it's important to listen more, talk less, and be a better observer.

The third type of awareness is organizational awareness. This has a lot to do with understanding group and organizational dynamics. We periodically find that otherwise successful people don't assimilate well into new roles because they don't pick up on how things are done in the new organization or they rely on how things were done where they came from. It's hard to successfully adapt to a new place without knowing how people operate and situations are handled.

People who take our assessments tend to fall in one of two camps. Those who are high on self-awareness are generally not surprised by what they see, and the scores validate their self-perceptions. These people tend to do a lot of thinking, evaluating, and challenging themselves. Those who are less self-aware don't think as much about their own thoughts and feelings and tend to be more surprised by what they see. In any event, having objective data can be very informative and motivating for those that are working on improving.

In my experience, I have found women to be higher in self-awareness than men. PRADCO, through much research on the similarities and differences of men and women, has discovered women tend to be more reflective, harder on themselves, and personalize things more than men. The reason for this may be early socialization in large part—how we were raised, the roles we play; but it's not only gender-specific. We work with a lot of men who are very self-aware and women who aren't. There are just more cases of the opposite being true.

We have also found that younger generations are more reflective than the older ones. They are more focused on what they want, what they need, and what they see for themselves; whereas with the more senior generations, people tend to do what needs to be done. This ties in with the work Simon Sinek is doing about the "power of why" and people wanting to have a purpose. Previously, the purpose of work was to pay your bills, do a job, and take care of your family. Now, there's a lot more focus on inner drive, mastery, and satisfaction.

That said, men and older generations are not doomed to a life of self-ignorance. People can develop their awareness through self-assessment or from getting feedback from other people. Asking questions and soliciting feedback are two very important and effective strategies, as they help people realize how they come across to others and what they can do differently. Often, a 360-degree feedback tool can be very useful for improving awareness. When someone who isn't self-aware comes for coaching, their journey to self-awareness is more guided by us but informed by others.

There are some people who just aren't aware at all, even in the face of feedback. I recently had a feedback session with a person where I was sharing our data. I was providing examples and reflecting what I had seen from our interaction that supported where the person's blind spots were. The person was not getting it. While I believe it's ideal to help people get there gently, if they don't, sometimes just being honest and giving good, tangible examples of things can help. Getting someone to become self-aware is crucial to a journey of personal development; the journey cannot be successful without it.

Luckily, most people can improve their awareness. In the cases where someone struggles, we give examples and hope they move the needle a little bit. The vast majority of the time, people can get it when it's pointed out in a positive way. However, if someone is not open to the feedback they get during these sessions, the problem isn't awareness but defensiveness.

Somebody who's thin-skinned will personalize their feedback and feel badly about it, but they may still accept it and work on it. Defensiveness is characterized by "it's not my problem, it's theirs" or "I can't help it because of this, these are the reasons why it's that way." In thinking about where defensiveness comes from, it usually stems from insecurity or lack of confidence and not knowing what to do differently. The reason we have a thriving coaching business is because our message is that most people are willing to get better; they just don't know what to do. People may have given them feedback and told them they're not good at this or that, but often they have not been told what to do instead.

One way to deal with defensiveness and eliminate it as a roadblock is to go back to what someone wants to achieve—their stated goals, and what they want to get out of this journey. Ask them if what they are becoming defensive about is, in fact, something they want to work on.

If a person isn't seeing it, of if they don't believe that it is significant enough to work on, then I'm not going to push it. My job is not to convince them, but to help them achieve what they want to improve upon. But I will bring everything back to what their overall objective is...if they want to get promoted, have a better relationship with their boss, or be a better leader, and if it is important to their overall objective. If making a change will help them accomplish the objective, people generally try. If they don't want to address a particular issue, and if it isn't going to impede the accomplishment of the goal, we can always work on something different.

Additionally, sometimes when people lack awareness, it's simply because they haven't spent much time or energy thinking about themselves. Rather, they are more "other" or "task" focused. They aren't deliberately ignoring it because they do not know it is there. The reality is that some people have never thought about what they need to improve.

One way to improve the success of a development journey is to include 360-degree feedback. PRADCO's QuickView™ 360 is a great tool to identify blind spots and get a new view of how we are perceived by others. One of the distinct advantages of 360-degree feedback is getting input from different groups of people. This includes soliciting feedback from peers, direct reports, and bosses. Often, we behave differently with different groups of people. For example, a leader might be supportive and helpful with her team because she feels that's her role. But with her peers, she doesn't offer them the same niceties, or maybe she doesn't choose her words as carefully—she's more blunt with peers because she feels they should be able to take it.

When feedback is solicited from people at different levels, it allows collaboration to occur. I may think I'm being supportive but somebody else thinks that I'm being too soft. Or, I think I'm being persuasive, but others see it as being dominant. Getting feedback allows us a different view of ourselves, as well as the ability to change people's perceptions. And, after all, perception is reality.

Improvement Orientation

If awareness is the first step on a journey of personal development, having an improvement orientation is the second. After you discover what you need to work on, you have a choice—do you want to make a change, or not?

There has been an evolution of coaching in the industry where, before, it was for problems and people who needed to be 'fixed'. Now, coaching has a much more positive connotation. It is something afforded to high-potential people and good performers. Even professional athletes have coaches, so engaging in self-improvement with direction from others can be very enlightening.

People who are initially self-aware are more open to change and improvement, but it is important to keep in mind people change at different paces. Normally, when we do our programs, they span a period of six to nine months. Roughly 80 percent of the people are on board from the beginning. It takes a meeting or two to build rapport— maybe they have some anxiety until they get a little more comfortable with what we're doing. For other people, though, it takes longer. It might be the second or the third meeting before real awareness and behavior change occurs.

When I encountered people who weren't immediately engaged, I used to think the person wasn't going to get it, didn't care about it, or wasn't open to change. But as time went on, some of the people would get it a little later. Maybe they needed a little more time to drop their defenses and have the feedback penetrate through their tougher exterior. Then, there is the moment of truth when people turn a corner and start making progress.

It is satisfying when people make a self-discovery. They are grateful for the feedback and the help, and can start making a change. That's been a huge satisfier for me in my career, to really help people overcome barriers.

One important element of this improvement-oriented mindset is internal locus of control. There are two types of locus of control: internal and external.

With an internal locus of control, one believes he or she can manage outcomes through one's own actions or decisions. For example, if someone with an internal locus of control fails a test, they may say, "I should have studied harder" or "I should have taken better notes in class."

A person with an external locus of control tends to believe outcomes are influenced by circumstances, other people, or even luck. For example, if someone with an external locus of control fails a test, they may say, "This professor always makes the tests too hard" or "I wasn't feeling well that day."

From a developmental perspective, it's best to look inside and have an internal locus of control because you can only change yourself. You may not be able to change a situation, but you can change the way you think about it. Someone who's defensive, resistant, or closed-minded only hurts themselves—they can't benefit from feedback which inhibits their ability to be maximally successful. Fortunately, there are shades of gray and people can shift their focus and the way they look at things.

I had an interesting experience not long ago. I was coaching a young woman whose boss would regularly tell her that she's defensive. That was his perception, but she didn't feel defensive and our assessment didn't show her to be defensive either. Interestingly, I hadn't experienced her as defensive, but nor did she actively give me the feeling she was accepting what I was saying. That's very different than being defensive.

We talked about how she's very even tempered and guarded, doesn't give any cues that she's listening, nor does she take any notes. She doesn't take notes because she's smart, has an excellent memory and doesn't need them. I explained to her that although her boss was labeling her behavior as defensive, in reality she was just failing to openly support and acknowledge what he was saying.

This was a huge breakthrough. Now, this woman has a way to reframe his feedback and understand where he was getting this impression of defensiveness. She has since gone back to clarify that she really wasn't trying to be defensive, but that she now realized what she was doing (or not doing) that was giving him that impression. Interestingly, a common positive byproduct of coaching is that communication can go a long way toward improving situations and relationships. In this case, she was able to take what she learned, change her own behavior, and also communicate with her boss to get them on a better path.

One reason we have encountered so little resistance to our coaching at PRADCO is because coaching these days is much more positive and proactive than it is punitive or problem-oriented. Most people who come for coaching are happy about it. They might have some nervousness about it, but they see it as an opportunity. Even people sent to us because they're "in trouble" feel like this is a chance to get better. It doesn't benefit anybody to be resentful toward us when we can be the way out of a problem or a way to a better opportunity. However, most people are sent to us for leadership development as a positive investment. And that's a shift in the times.

Twenty years ago, that wasn't the case. Organizations weren't investing in people for positive reasons, or even for succession planning. It was more problem focused. This shift started when people realized that there were senior leaders planning to retire and lots of younger people who were going to have to lead but didn't really know how. Today, coaching has become more developmental as opposed to problem-oriented, which I think allows people to be more change-oriented and open to the opportunity.

The shift in coaching has been positive, and we have a much greater likelihood of success. So, when customers ask if people really do change, our answer is a resounding "Yes".

Commitment to Change

People have different levels of resistance to coaching but, often, once a trusting relationship is developed, they will be more improvement oriented and open to change. Typically, this includes focusing time and energy on personal development.

One of the best pieces of feedback we get from our programs is people are appreciative of time to focus on themselves. Otherwise, people just go through their days responding to emails and sitting in meetings. Change and improvement require focused time. It also requires changing habits that may be interfering in one's success. Often, people know what their problems are, but they don't know what to do instead. Figuring this out and developing new habits can lead to positive change and better outcomes.

Once a person knows what to do, however, they need to be committed to doing it and working on it every day, if not multiple times a day.

One of the books we refer to a lot when coaching is "The Power of Habit," by Charles Duhigg. It discusses the neurological elements of why we do what we do. To change a habit requires rewiring your brain, and that requires exhibiting different behaviors. Habits can't really be extinguished until they are replaced by new ones.

We typically help people define three or four goals, things that they want to work on. We focus heavily on behaviors, because no matter what you think or what you feel, if you behave differently, you will have a different outcome, which then changes your thoughts and feelings in kind of a cyclical way.

Also, repetition and practice are very important to changing your behavior. Changing behavior takes a long time and a lot of commitment. When we work with somebody for a month or two, it's unlikely that there will be a significant, long lasting change. But with touchpoints over the course of six months, for example, people get to practice, develop new habits, and they get some reinforcement.

Personally, I have made a lot of changes over the years to be a more effective leader. It has taken a lot of hard work and commitment. My most eye-opening moment, demonstrating my need for change, came from my first 360.

I've always been an assertive person, and felt that it was a good thing. That is why I got into leadership roles and people listened and followed my lead. When I did my first 360, I scored in the 99th percentile on the scale of Dominant—I was at the very top, according to every person who rated me.

Unfortunately for me, the goal of a 360 is not consistency, but variety. People want and need different levels of things from their coworkers. It was eye-opening because it was extreme, not because it was there. I always knew I was dominant, but it was too much of a good thing. This feedback helped me understand why some things weren't going well...this person wasn't happy working for me, or this person wasn't receptive. They might have done what I asked, but they weren't engaged. Ever since then, I've had an appreciation for moderation and for situational leadership. It was career and life changing for me. And that was something that didn't just change overnight.

When I'm working with someone who possesses a similar dominant style, it can be discouraging for them because it's hard to change. We have found the best way to attack this problem is to frame it as an overused strength that can be backed down with practice. After empathizing a bit, I share some things that have worked for me and others that have been too reliant on the dominant lever, and which can neutralize the situation and give people hope that they will be able to make a move without losing their true self.

I also often tell people (and remind myself) that it's an error in the right direction. It's a lot easier to back dominance down than it is to take somebody who's very low and get them to be more dominant to an acceptable level. But that doesn't mean it's easy. People must be motivated to change and determined to keep working on it. And to make it even more difficult, one slip can definitely be a setback.

Another thing to keep in mind is that it's important to make changes while still being authentic. If a person is going to make a change, it should

27

be a matter of degree rather than a wholesale change. For example, I will always be dominant. That's a personality trait that I have, but I can be other things too. Maybe I need to be more cooperative and collaborative, which by doing so will lower my dominance. Things need to balance out. It may not even be making a change to assertiveness, but simply working harder to make cooperation and collaboration more of a priority.

To succeed on a journey of personal development and have successful behavior changes, development goals need to be at the forefront of the mind. To keep it there, it helps to have distributed practice and learning over time. Part of our coaching model at PRADCO is to meet with people over a six-to-nine-month period, once a month. This gives the lessons duration; we want to be able to come back to it and have the learning build on itself. Repeated visits take a lot of dedication, but lasting change takes commitment and repeated practice.

Almost all our development programs include a behavioral assessment. The Quick View Leadership Assessment measures 50 behaviors, or "tools" that can be used. Once you acknowledge them, you have them at your disposal. You can be dominant, or you can be cooperative; you can be persuasive, or you can be supportive. It just depends on what the situation calls for. It's a process of evolution, really, and it's important to become comfortable with the tools in the toolbox and with knowing when to use them.

It's easy to fall back on what comes naturally, which may not be the best approach. It's natural to fall back on being assertive, especially in stressful times. But to know that other tools will work just as well (or better) and maybe have fewer negative consequences is a great thing to acknowledge and remember in these situations.

Decide What You Want Your Brand to Be

When setting goals for a personal journey of development, it's important for people to have a good understanding of how they want to be perceived, as well as what they want their brand to be. Once that is determined, people can take actions to create the light in which they want to be viewed by others. People are judgers. They draw their conclusions based on what they think. And if you don't know how people experience you, or you don't know what they think about you, then you're not able to control that perception. The following example demonstrates the power of perception and controlling your brand.

PRADCO has been in business since 1955, and over that time frame, we have become excellent assessors and capable psychologists. I had a few customers over the years who have given me some noteworthy feedback. They felt our tools and reports were excellent, our people were better than the rest, and our assessments among the most accurate in the industry.

However, our materials didn't look very good. Our reports weren't fancy or colorful, and some people wouldn't choose us because we weren't marketing oriented. We had a lot of text but not a lot of graphics or visually pleasing elements. We were capable psychologists writing accurate reports, but we were still missing out on some work. I have been fortunate to develop some really great relationships with consultants and HR leaders over the years, and one person in particular was brutally honest about our deliverables. He told me (often) that if we were to make our reports more aesthetically pleasing, and if we would jazz up our corporate brand a bit, we would have much more success winning business. While people may have been making buying decisions based on a superficial quality, being open to this feedback put us in a position to change our approach to still be capable and accurate, but to have our brand look and be better at the same time.

Once we recognized the perception people had of our materials and made some changes, things improved.

On a more personal level, consider this example: I'm a Ph.D. psychologist, and pretty guarded as a person. I don't have a high need for relationships, nor do I want much recognition. I'm more of an introverted person at heart.

But having a degree, being a psychologist, being formal in my interactions with people, and running a company would likely intimidate some people. They wouldn't think I was very friendly, and they could misread my cues. People weren't relating to me like I wanted them to.

Being a self-aware person who thinks about things a lot, I wanted to be perceived differently and I wanted to have more fun with what I was doing. I decided (with the help of some friends) that I could still be respected as a business owner and as a leader, but be a bit more natural and truer to my real self. Once I recognized that, I made a deliberate effort to be friendlier, go to more social events, and be more open. I found I didn't have to be in this shell, and I could become more versatile. I dressed casually much more often (and still do) and am more willing to be open with others.

These changes have made a huge difference. So, when I show up as a formal, analytical doctor, people respond one way; when I show up as a business owner who's relatable, open and vulnerable, they respond in a completely different way—and on a much more personal level. I had the ability and opportunity to change how people responded to me by changing how I presented myself to others. Over the years, I've really noticed that I connect with people more naturally and our company has a better reputation because of what I do and the culture we're building. And so, continues my and our company's journey of development.

Your brand is more than just how you dress, it's the words that you use and your communication style. One of the best ways to make someone feel comfortable with you is to mirror them. It's important to mirror or match the person you're with. If they are more formal, they won't want you to walk in five minutes late, using slang, and wearing flip-flops. But if they are more casual, they won't be as comfortable if you speak in clipped tones and refuse to talk about anything personal while wearing a suit with a dress shirt buttoned up to the collar.

This is not to say you should completely change your brand to match the person you are with. But, like being able to be dominant or laid-back depending on the situation, mirroring and slightly altering your presence is an approach that can make interactions more pleasant for everyone involved.

A lot of the work we do involves helping people develop their presence and have more impact. One model we use was developed by Albert Mehrabian, a professor from UCLA who has done a great deal of work on the relative importance of verbal and nonverbal messages. According to Mehrabian, there are three elements of impact: verbal, vocal, and visual.

Verbal impact is what you say and how you say it. Vocal impact is how you sound, including loudness and inflection. Visual impact is how you look; your clothes, your materials, your posture, etc. Knowing where a person is strong and where someone is weak can lead to different behaviors to have more impact.

As I mentioned earlier, it's important to understand your own style and the styles of others. Once awareness is there, it's up to you to make changes and adjust to the other person. You want to understand their style, but it's not up to them to change. You can only control what you do and if you change or not. Knowing how the brand you project tends to affect others is something that people need to be aware of. And developing and improving one's impact is a common thing we work on to help people be more effective.

Generational differences are also important in positioning one's brand. People in prior generations didn't need to be as versatile because of who they managed and "acceptable" styles of management. The people I'm managing all have different styles and needs. As a leader, I need to use the tools that will be most effective for a given person. We regularly help people coach and motivate others more (and better), which is a huge generational difference. In prior generations, leaders needed to just say what they wanted done. The fear of being fired or replaced was motivation enough. But for the newer generations, motivation is necessary to generate results and have an engaged workforce.

It used to be that Driving Results was the most important behavior on the Quick View Leadership Assessment to get things done through others. Now, the number one thing good leaders do is motivate others. Leaders must determine how to bring out the very best in others. And, again, that's different; it used to be just telling people what to do—my old style. Today, I spend much more time relating to people, understanding what's important to them, and trying to figure out the best way to help them achieve their goals. Whether in a coaching engagement or with my own team, I really try to adapt to the situation and the person I am dealing with to get the best, most mutually beneficial outcome as possible.

One program we offer today is based on Personal Styles. It deals with understanding the different ways people interact and communicate with each other. If you've never been exposed to a program like this, it's hard to know how to classify and react to different types of people. A key point to the program is about modifying your own style as you can't change other people; all you can do is change how you operate. When we do the Personal Styles training, it's about helping you understand yourself and others so that you can make the necessary adjustments and adaptations. It also gives people a common language. People tend to relate to the material because it's fun, light, and no one style is better than another. The goal is to be versatile within your style so that you can easily adapt to people who are different.

It's typically worthwhile to spend a little time understanding who your audience is so an intentional plan can be made to successfully address them. For example, one of our consultants did Personal Styles training with a group of engineers. As a group, engineers tend to be analytical and introverted, so when presenting to that group, it was important to share data and be fact-based. They would not have been as receptive to jokes or lively group exercises, which would have inhibited learning and group interactions. Again, you can't control how others will react, but you can be intentional about how you address different people and situations.

Final Steps and Moving Forward

Once you know what you want to improve upon, it's a matter of making it happen. If working better with others is the goal, identify a few relationships that need work, and make a plan for those particular people. What do you have in common with them? What are the things that are important to them in life? What can you do with the person that would be rewarding to you and to them?

Figure out a targeted, measurable plan for those people and build specific action steps to make things better. And then, write it all down. By writing down what you're going to do, it's a commitment you must uphold. Revisit this a month later with your coach and see how you are doing. Did I do what I said I would do? Did it work? How could I go back again with a slightly different approach?

Not everything works the first time—or ever. Sometimes, it's trial and error. But typically, if you focus on something, make the change, and adjust over time, things will improve.

In this journey of personal development, resilience is key, as is keeping the focus on progress, not perfection. Things aren't going to be perfect. You don't have to go from 1 to 100; you just need to make small incremental steps. Resilience complements an improvement orientation. If you're improvement oriented, it's important to be resilient because you may get a message you don't like. You're going to come upon an obstacle that you can't master, but it's all a journey—and that's what is most important.

One additional point: How you bounce back from setbacks is also important. In my own personal experience, what I have been able to achieve is, in large part, due to people who were doubters or who pointed out weaknesses in me.

Early on in my career, I had a peer who would point out my flaws and areas of inexperience on a regular basis. He would point out that I wasn't contributing to sales, wasn't good at reading financials, or that I was too dominant, and people didn't love working for me. He was largely right, so with my focus on being better, I always looked for what I could do differently. My response was not to get mad or discouraged. Instead, I set out to learn and practice the things I need to improve upon. As time went on, I started to get relatively good at those things, just because I didn't want to have those weaknesses. The feedback wasn't delivered in the spirit of positivity, but it motivated me to do better and become much more well-rounded.

In summary, I have been on a journey of personal development without even realizing it. As a competitive, driven type of person I want to be successful personally and as a leader at PRADCO, and it's definitely a work in progress. I have been blessed with many opportunities in my life, and as a psychologist I have been a student of human behavior, leadership development, and successful businesses. I have found it helpful to take feedback from any source, regardless of how it has been given, and just try to be better. Each day is a challenge, and I try to leave my job each day feeling that I did better today than I did yesterday or the day before. With resilience and an eye toward the future, I attempt to look inward and take a step toward the light each day. It takes time and energy, but it has been worth it for me.

If you're ready to take your own journey, all you need to do is take the first step. That step can be to develop your own awareness, get feedback from others, or to make meaningful change a goal. It is achievable, and it is rewarding to make progress, even when it is difficult. It's not easy, but the results are very rewarding.

Kristin Tull

Over the past 27 years, Dr. Kristin Tull has taken on significant challenges during her ascension to the Presidency of PRADCO, a women-owned organization that specializes in helping companies select, develop and retain people who fit their cultures and contribute to organizational goals. In addition to her account management and business development activities, Kristin has been an industry leader in the creation and validation of the assessment instruments that constitute the backbone of PRADCO's evaluation and development strategy.

While building her own team of management consultants, Kristin has worked extensively with high-level executives in some of PRADCO's largest clients. She spearheads PRADCO's investigative work into identifying differences among organizational cultures and demographic populations. Most recently, Kristin has focused her efforts on the creation and delivery of a dual-track coaching program, offering a structured, yet flexible approach to developing high-potential performers. She is also very involved with, and passionate about developing women leaders.

Kristin earned her B.A. in Psychology at Denison University, her M.A. in Clinical Psychology at Xavier University, and her Ph.D. in Industrial/Organizational Psychology at the University of Akron. She is a Licensed Psychologist in the State of Ohio.

Authenticity in the Workplace
LEE ANN COCHRAN

Do you remember a moment when you engaged with an authentic person? The way they made you feel? The desire to spend more time with them in the future? I certainly do. When I spend time with my early career mentor, it leaves me feeling comfortable and complete. It surfaces feelings which inspires me to have more impact on the world. Our interactions allow me to be vulnerable and honest. I know that he has my best interests at heart and always has others' well-being in mind. I often feel complete after an interaction like this.

Alternatively, I have had interactions with inauthentic people. It is a completely different experience.

How do you know if someone is authentic? For me it is around eye contact, how much of their attention I receive, the dialogue they engage with, and how they make me feel. During a challenging point in my career I had regular interactions with an inauthentic person, and it drove me to move on to new opportunities.

It was evident that no matter how I interacted with this person, the outcome would never be consistent or valuable. At the end of inauthentic interactions, I often feel tired, drained, and confused.

Authenticity is defined by Meriam-Webster's Dictionary as "Not false or imitation: real, actual; true to one's own personality, spirit, or character."

This seems so simple; so black and white: Be true to yourself.

But like most things, it is easier said than done. True authenticity is more nuanced than the dictionary definition and starts with being honest to yourself. It requires understanding who you truly are, and being true to what you discover.

Being truly authentic also means accepting that who you are today is not ultimately who you will aspire to be. You must be willing to do what it takes to achieve it.

The first step is knowing who you are. Then, once you know, being authentic to your true self 100 percent of the time—no matter what situation you find yourself in. If you can't be comfortable in your own skin, you will never feel fulfilled in your personal and professional life. Rather, you'll continue to wear a façade.

Just as important, you cannot affect change unless you know what it is that you want to change. Learn to identify where you are not authentic and you can begin to understand why inauthenticity negatively impacts yourself, as well as those around you. Also, this holds true at home, with friends or family, or even in the workplace. Once you recognize what changes to make, you've taken a critical step toward authenticity.

Therein lies the ultimate challenge: How to achieve your true authentic self?

On the pages that follow, I hope to not only help you identify your authentic self, but also share how to understand authenticity and recognize it in others. You'll learn from examples of what it looks like and how it's applied. I'll provide insight about the dangers of inauthenticity, reveal a series of roadblocks which serve as the enemies of change, and offer advice on how to overcome these barriers to achieve authenticity.

In addition, I'll share the results of an authenticity survey undertaken to get at the root of how people see themselves when it comes to authenticity, as well as how they are striving to improve. My hope is that when you've finished, you will have embraced change and be on your way to achieving your true authentic self.

Recognizing Authenticity in Yourself and Others

You can recognize authenticity in other people by the way they make you feel when you're with them. When you are with someone genuine, you feel relaxed. There's nothing fake on either side. You can be yourself; they can be themselves; and there is a genuine connection.

When someone is being authentic, they talk about a variety of subjects—not just the standard "Do you have a family?" "What's the weather like?" or other small talk before segueing to "OK, now let's get to the meeting". You have the type of conversation which offers a sense of what makes the other person tick: what interests them, how they treat people, etc.

In the workplace, you can recognize authentic people by your ability to forge a genuine connection with them. And, beyond conversation, watch how people treat others at all levels of the organization—what you see reveals a lot about them.

For example, if I see someone who ignores the cleaning staff when they come into the office to pick up a garbage can, that says a lot about the type of person he or she is. Everyone deserves to be welcomed. When you see someone engage in conversation on a meaningful basis, that is a person who is authentic.

You can also recognize authenticity by the way someone shakes your hand, says 'hello', or whether they make eye contact when you meet them. Non-verbal cues often tell a lot about people. You're able to tell if someone is excited to see you or meet you, or if they're simply checking a box: "Greeted them by shaking their hand... check. Now, move along."

If your authentic self doesn't match the culture of your workplace, you may find yourself in a negative work environment—uncomfortable and being inauthentic just to get by. Let's say your authenticity includes pushing the envelope with colleagues or asking tough questions. If you find yourself in a very tight, buttoned-up environment, it may become difficult to be authentic because you're constantly trying to keep the "real" you inside. When that happens, to be authentic you'd need to do one of two things: find a new job with a different workplace where you're more comfortable in your own skin being a little louder and more colorful or having a frank conversation with the leadership team on who you are. For the authentic individual, being able to stay in this type of environment depends completely on how open leadership is to you releasing your authentic self.

Here's another example, albeit an extreme one: In your workplace, can you put a picture of your family on your desk?

I'm sure you're saying to yourself, "Self, that doesn't seem extreme!"

Well, what if that family picture has two women, and a blended family of children who are adopted and/or biological, and not everyone looks the same?

If not, and your workplace would only allow that family photo if it's a standard man, woman, and white picket fence family, are you really being authentic? Someone once told me how hard it was to go to work each day because they didn't have that "standard" family and knew they couldn't talk about their "real" family at work.

This then becomes one litmus test on your authenticity in the workplace.

There are other, less important, examples of authenticity at work. Likely, being able to show your family is much more important than whether you can easily laugh at work, make jokes and in general enjoy time with colleagues. How much laughter and enjoyment you have at work is a great measure for how authentic you can be.

This is where working in an environment different from who you are means some measure of compromise between you and your employer. How much laughter you have at work may not be all that important to you, but it demonstrates how you can still be authentic yet know where to draw the line. Authenticity isn't an absolute when it comes to straddling personal and professional life—if it were, we'd only be able to work for ourselves!

Despite this, recognizing authenticity can be challenging. People want to be themselves, but there are barriers that keep them from doing so, as well as internal struggles that take place every day.

At one of my previous employers, an 80-plus-year-old company, our leadership team was primarily comprised of white males from the defense industry. They didn't do "change" well, which made it challenging for me to be authentic because I like to think outside the box. My previous boss asked me to innovate—that was part of my job. But, I was asked to innovate within a structure of meetings and hierarchies which included many barriers as my day-to-day parameters. When I eventually concluded that while I loved my work, the risk of working in a place where I was forced to compromise too much of my authenticity would be to start losing my authenticity through complacency.

Ask yourself the same questions in the workplace and see whether you can recognize your own authenticity as well as those around you.

After surveying close to 100 people, the importance of authenticity in the workplace proved itself with this quote: "Authenticity is very important to me in all aspects of my life. I used to try to fit whatever mold was expected of me depending on the situation, and it was exhausting. Now that I have learned to be my authentic self, while still maintaining situational awareness, I am a much more relaxed and content person."

Similarly, I heard this as well: "It shows transparency and integrity. People know what they get with you. You can be trusted and relied upon. Furthermore, people are more likely to follow an authentic person."

Each of these leads to a series of business results you can achieve by being authentic.

Understanding Authenticity

Part of authenticity is trying to understand and be accommodating of other people's authentic selves—you want them to accept you, so you must accept them.

45

For example, I wouldn't automatically feel comfortable coming into a meeting and swearing a lot—that's not who I really am. But, if the people I was meeting with were swearing, I would just go with the flow and think, "Wow they have a pretty progressive culture here. That's awesome if that's how they get their work done. More power to them."

Conversely, you can feel a difference when people try to use different words or talk about a subject they don't really know. If I were to come into the same meeting and try to curse and be more brash than I usually feel comfortable doing, it would quickly become obvious to those people that I was being fake. This would make them feel uncomfortable around me because they would know I was inauthentic.

Another example would be if you didn't know very much about a topic being discussed and tried to pretend you did. People notice. And, yes, there is a difference between saying, "I'm just learning about this subject, and the language is new to me" and then participating in the conversation versus just blowing smoke by pretending to be a subject matter expert after a day or so of research.

In the survey, I found consistency in that authentic people demonstrate confidence. They are not fearful of learning and developing from others. One person stated, "The person seems at ease, is not trying to impress or remind you of their importance and is fully engaged in the conversation or subject at hand."

We run into a lot of people in the workplace and in our personal lives who are superficial and inauthentic when they don't want to connect with you or don't really care what they're doing. These people are just checking that box. But there are others who are really just "surface"-level authentic—and it's because of the environment they're in rather than whether they are trying to be someone else.

For example, let's say you're working in the fast-food environment. You are giving a lot of service to others—taking orders, collecting money, delivering food. There are not really a lot of different ways to be excited about the work. You are pleasant, you smile, you make eye contact. You do the things you're supposed to do, but there is no excitement behind your actions. In this case, you're not just checking a box. You are being authentic on the "surface". People in this type of situation are not inauthentic. More likely, they're just not authentically happy in their jobs.

One concern around this is the exhaustion you feel in being inauthentic all day long. As one survey respondent said, "I come away feeling empty and used and without purpose."

The challenge with this scenario is how an organization can achieve long-term results if their employees leave feeling drained and not replenished.

The Importance of the Authentic Self

If being authentic to your true self in the workplace sounds like a lot of work, that's because most of the time it is. Sometimes, it seems as if it would be easier to simply be one of many; to go with the flow and be whomever your boss and/or your co-workers want you to be.

This is being disingenuous to yourself.

Think about it: You spend 40-plus hours each week at work. Theoretically, a decent amount of that time is spent with your co-workers. If you can't be "you" for at least half of your waking hours, you will wear yourself out by pretending to be someone you're not. Day by day, week by week, month by month, and year by year, the grind of putting on that façade—and keeping it on all day long—will become much harder than simply slowing down, figuring out who you really are, and working on being true to that.

Have you every laughed or smiled so much that your cheeks hurt? I'm talking about real laughs and real smiles. Now, have you ever fake smiled and fake laughed so much that you give yourself a pounding headache that lasts for hours?

I'll take the painful cheeks every time.

Why?

Because eventually, I'll stop smiling. My cheeks will return to normal, but the feeling of happiness will remain. Conversely, when I stop fake smiling and pretending to enjoy myself, the headache will still be there. And, I'll probably be exhausted, too.

This is the difference between finding and being true to your authentic self and just faking your way through the day, every day. The former may involve a bit of short-term pain. But it results in long-term gain across every aspect of your life. The latter? Well, you may avoid awkwardness and potentially some discomfort in your office—as well as your personal life—but you're giving up an awful lot. Ultimately, it will result in a long-term detriment to your well-being.

If you have the chance, I strongly recommend typing the words "Stanford marshmallow experiment" into a search engine and clicking on the links. You'll read about a study that analyzed the human nature of delayed gratification and the results: enduring current unpleasantness for a greater reward in the future.

Ultimately, the long-term benefit of being true to your authentic self is that you will end up being a happy person with few regrets. You will have lived an awesome life because you weren't afraid to try new things. You will have taken risks. And, you will have always tried to make decisions that were the best or most beneficial to your authentic self. It will lead to a sense of fulfillment in life.

That said, being authentic won't pave the way to automatic economic success—you won't become a millionaire or suddenly get the promotion to CEO just by being authentic. Rather, if you DO achieve that level of success, you will enjoy it more by being authentic instead of living behind a façade. It's safe to say that there are few people who, near the end of their lives, look back and say, "I'm glad I stayed at that job where I was miserable so I could die with more money." Instead, they're more likely to say, "I wish I had left that miserable job so I could have spent more time with my family," or "I wish I had left that miserable job and found something that I truly enjoyed."

But wouldn't it be better to reflect back and say, "I'm happy I was always true to myself—through the good times and the bad."

The Downside of Inauthenticity

Being inauthentic carries with it numerous downsides—a few of which we've discussed. But another is that it drains you—and those around you. And, because either you or those around you are being drained, you become disconnected.

For example, you don't allow other to see your authentic self, so you become that aloof employee who comes in, doesn't talk to anyone, does their job, and leaves the office at 4:59 p.m. each day. You're pretty much disconnected from your co-workers.

Or, you come in, maintain the façade, and drain people's energy because they must deal with the fake you.

Either way, your inauthenticity creates a negative impact on yourself and those around you. Worse, it wears you down. You dread going to work because it takes a lot of energy to put up and keep the façade. It takes a lot of energy to disassociate yourself with those around you— or conversely, to associate in an inauthentic way with those around you. You begin to live for the weekends, when you don't have to deal with anyone else at work.

You end up making no real connections.

At home, you might have the same problems if you're inauthentic there. I've read about this happening with people who get married young. They mature and change over the years, but perhaps not together. If they're not authentic to themselves and their spouse, they can't be open to each other's changes. Then, they discover they can't be who they really are when they are in their own house.

People who are inauthentic at home and at work become trapped by their own inauthenticity. Later in life, it's something they come to regret.

In 2002, a psychological study in the Journal of Personality and Social Psychology called "The inaction effect in the psychology of regret" found people regret inaction more than action. This has a direct correlation to being authentic. When you're not "you", you come to regret it.

And this goes well beyond the research laboratory. The popular YouTube video, *What's Your Biggest Regret (Nobody Wants to Admit the Biggest One of All)* (https://www.youtube.com/watch?v=R45HcYA8uRA) really hammers this point home.

The video creators placed a chalkboard in the middle of New York City. They wrote a single question across the top: What's your biggest regret? And then they left it there for a full day.

This open-ended question produced a variety of answers, but they all had one thing in common: they all were something that the person did not do but they wish they had. For example, some people wished they had taken a trip. Others wrote they wish they had said "I love you" more. Others regretted not going back to school.

Taken together, it's interesting to think to be happy and have no (or at least fewer) big regrets, we should be taking risks and trying to fulfill ourselves. When we look back over our lives, it will be the things that we didn't do that jump out at us.

One person wrote "Not following my dreams." Very succinct!

Pursuing dreams is one of the purest forms of being true to our authentic selves. Instead of spending an entire day trying to convince yourself that you love what you are doing while wishing you were out doing something else, go out and try to do that something else!

Just like there is no guarantee you will become a millionaire, there is no guarantee you will achieve your dream. Trying, failing, and finding a new dream is better than spending your entire life wondering, "What if ..." A wise man one said, you miss all the shots you don't take.

Another downside to inauthenticity is it drains your ability to be courageous. If you're not authentic, you're already sacrificing some courage. So, it becomes easier to go ahead and pass on other things that require courage. One example is you won't say anything controversial or contrarian to those around you. Personally, I have all sorts of crazy ideas I want to do. One was writing this section of the book. I still remember having to put together my plan for having a conversation about writing this section with my husband. I anticipated him saying, "Why this? Why now? Why the investment?"

I had to be ready to answer those questions and be authentic about the reasons for each.

After surveying more than 100 people about their thoughts on authenticity, I only came across one person who believed it was not possible to be inauthentic. The data revealed that nearly 30 percent of people struggle with being their authentic self. It's a challenge they wake up every day to face.

Impact on Self

When someone is inauthentic, their stress levels rise. As mentioned earlier, they dread going into the office and having to be someone fake—often, without realizing how and why they're doing it.

You smile less. You interact with people less. And you become a weaker team player.

Once, with a former employer I was working on a project where the team wasn't a happy environment. One of the team members was sort of a bulldog—he had trouble playing nice with others. He didn't treat people with respect and didn't emulate the core values we espoused at that organization.

It was hard to work with this person because I didn't like the way he treated others. But, I knew I had a job to do and milestones to reach. Therefore, I had to find a delicate balance between being direct and being kind to him, allowing us to move the project forward. I had to consciously try to not be fake, but still rein in my authentic self. I created that compromise with myself: I decided I would stand up for those people he treated wrong. But, if his attitude and actions were just normal, negative energy, I would ignore them and just focus on the job.

By doing so, I noticed a gradual difference in myself. I began dreading to wake up on the days I had meetings with that team. I was slower to get out of bed. I wasn't excited about going to work. I stopped greeting my husband with a smile on my face when I returned from work.

Defying my true authentic self and going along with the co-worker's attitude negatively impacted me. I recognized the difference.

When making these types of compromises, you will need to decide what you can live with, not waste time ruminating on it and refuse to compromise further.

In my case, I knew I needed to be genuine to myself in choosing how to behave with him. I also knew it would be unfair to me—and others—if I allowed him to continually cross lines. I realized if I was too passive, I would be upset with myself. If I was too aggressive, I would create an environment too uncomfortable for the rest of my time. So that healthy balance—a little bit of discomfort by holding him accountable for his actions that crossed the line—allowed me to live with myself and for us to move the project forward.

Being authentic allows you to reach those compromises where you feel you could be comfortable and not make you angry with yourself. It won't ruin your entire day or even week. Keep in mind, this isn't easy to figure out. In my case, it required numerous conversations with my husband and various co-workers to figure out where to draw the line. Putting authenticity compromises into action is challenging in the workplace because you do have a career—and potential future promotions—to consider. Nobody benefits from a victory just for victory's sake.

But, it's been proven that companies with happy, engaged and content employees are more successful than those which don't. The former employees invest their energies in productive work rather than wasting it pretending to be someone they are not.

Once more, being authentic allows people to feel comfortable around you. Think of it like a good therapist: you can walk in and meet them, and soon you'll be letting your guard down to talk. Think of inauthenticity as being more closed off. You never really get to the heart of the matter, and if you do, it takes much too long.

At its core, being inauthentic compromises your ability to develop stronger work relationships, achieve satisfaction at work, and be a productive member of the team.

Choosing Authenticity

Choosing authenticity means cultivating the courage to be emotionally honest, setting boundaries and allowing ourselves to be vulnerable. It means exercising the compassion that comes from knowing we are all made of strength and struggle and connected to each other through a loving and resilient human spirit. An authentic person nurtures that connection and establishes a sense of belonging. This can only happen when he or she lets go of what they are told they are supposed to be and embraces who they really are.

When we make the choice to choose authenticity it can lead to a more fulfilling life. This can allow for more intimate relationships, stronger work results and more impact in the activities you take on. One person among those surveyed explained how they choose authenticity in a tough environment: "Mostly by trying to show my kind and caring side instead of the harsh exterior that my profession usually espouses."

It is important to recognize when you are being authentic because it's a muscle, and you need to practice consistency. Think of it like weight training. If you don't practice is correctly, you'll hurt yourself.

It is also important to understand that authenticity in the workplace begins with authenticity at home. If you're married or live with someone, you'll need a partner at home who is open and supportive.

Brené Brown stated, "Authenticity demands wholehearted living and loving—even when it's hard, even when we're wrestling with the fear of not being good enough, and especially when the joy is so intense that we're afraid to let ourselves feel it."

Although, it carries satisfaction with it.

Mindfully practicing authenticity during our most soul-searching struggles is how we invite grace, joy, and gratitude into our lives. As such, authenticity must be a daily practice, and practice is essential. Brené Brown clearly articulates how authenticity is a daily practice below. After reading this it became so clear to me why authenticity in the workplace is critical to so many people.

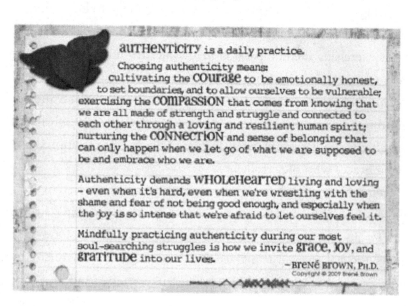

The Discomfort Factor

Achieving authenticity, as noted earlier, can at times feel a bit uncomfortable. If you're truly being yourself and strive for what you want, you push yourself. You reject the status quo and lay down a personal challenge. You ultimately seek—and aim to discover—the fire inside you. Again, this isn't easy. Start by doing things which are best for you rather than taking the path of least resistance. Remove toxic things from your life. Work in a healthy environment. Try to avoid people and situations which make you feel as if you cannot be happy or your authentic self.

This doesn't mean being authentic gives you a license to avoid doing things you don't want to do. Rather, being authentic is understanding you don't necessarily want to do something, but must to achieve something else you do want or need.

Enter the discomfort factor.

By facing discomfort, you learn how to do something you don't want to do and still be authentic. Through practice, you become able to make the most of a situation and eliminate any semblance of being fake because you have certainty in what it is you are striving to achieve.

On the surface, this may sound like you're doing things solely for yourself. But being authentic is not the same as being selfish—even if it may feel that way at first. Here's an example: Going to out with your spouse's friends.

OK. Some of you have great relationships with your spouse's friends, but many people do not. So maybe you do not get along with these friends or get replenished by them and going to dinner with them seems like a punishment. But, to make your partner happy, you go to dinner. It is all about finding a balance: How much can you bend while still being true to yourself?

Everyone has a different "line in the sand," as it were, and you need to find your authentic self to discover where to draw your own line. This requires something more than insight. It demands you to be strong.

Finding Strength

People often ask me how to be authentic without appearing to be weak?

This is common among people who are more amiable and often opt to go with the flow. This is also true for those new in their career, still working to have trust with the team. They believe that trying to be a leader while also being laid back makes you appear to be a pushover. But nothing could be further from the truth.

You can be authentic and still enforce deadlines, reprimand people, and hold them accountable. You can be, well, you, without having to put on a façade of a hard-nosed disciplinarian.

There is a fine line between delivering the duties of your job and being yourself. This is where empathy comes into play.

Empathy allows you to be strong without taking other people's emotions and actions on yourself. Instead, by displaying empathy, you allow your authenticity—and strength—to shine through. You are better able to draw a line in the sand while still understanding where that line should be. Empathy means you can relate to the others you're managing while still being yourself. By employing empathy, the last thing you'll look like to others is weak.

Embrace Change

A few years ago, one of my coaches said something to me that opened my eyes. He asked, "If you could change one thing you did this week, what would it be?"

At the time, I didn't understand the value of this question. Why would I want to talk about the things I wanted to change? It seemed such a negative thing to dwell upon.

Eventually, however, I realized he wanted me to recognize it was OK to have made those decisions and choices because they were opportunities to learn.

I came to understand he wanted me to change how I thought about my actions, choices, and decisions. And so, I processed it through a new lens. I saw I could avoid making the same mistakes in the future. It allowed me to see things differently—and approach everything with more authenticity than before. Looking back, without the ability to do this, I would not have been able to grow through my experiences.

It is important, therefore, to tell yourself when you are or have been your authentic self, and when you do something right, give yourself a dose of positive reinforcement. Catch yourself when you're being inauthentic or doing something wrong, and learn from those moments. It's far too easy to get caught up in the stress of daily life and work, and forget to say, "Good job. You're getting there."

Embracing change means taking a series of small steps in the right direction. Change requires diligence, consistency and action. When you embrace change to become your authentic self, it becomes a slow-but-steady chain reaction. Suddenly, people around you feel it, and they also can begin to be authentic.

Find the Benefits

One enormous benefit of authenticity in the workplace is retention. Every good manager knows training employees and hiring is one of the hardest things an organization does. When you finally assemble a good team, the last thing you want is to watch them leave.

When asked what you do when you are in a situation where you can not be your authentic self, there was consistency around a few key actions: silence, leave, withdraw and clam up.

None of these ultimately lead to workforce retention. Instead, these behaviors will leave employees not feeling valued, unmotivated, dissatisfied and ultimately looking for what is next.

At home, or in your personal life, one of the biggest benefits of authenticity is your ability to be one consistent person. When I run into a co-worker at a football game or out at a restaurant and I'm with my husband, I want to be the exact same person they run into in the hallway at work. By doing so, you never have to think about what version of yourself you were the last time you interacted with that person—whether face-to-face, in a meeting, or in a written email.

One example of something I struggle with all the time is that I am a stepmom. I'm my children's mother, but we are a blended family so they have another mom as well. That sounds simple, but it's actually very complicated. If you let inauthenticity creep in, it can be something of a Pandora's box.

Sometimes, when I say I am a stepmom, I get a question such as, "Well, when are you going to have your own kids?"

I'm not really sure how people automatically jump to that conclusion—that my step-kids aren't my own kids—but it happens more often than people think.

If I omit the part about being a stepmom and just mention I have kids, when they later find out I'm a stepmom, I get either a dismissive or accusatory remark that it means something less: "Well, you're their stepmom."

Instead, I found to be authentic, I would develop an elevator speech on our families. It allows me to feel that I won't have to explain, won't have to use qualifiers, and won't have to put on any façades about the situation.

I did this after learning how people get confused about what blended families are. But, in this day and age, there are so many blended families that it's common. Due to the lack of knowledge around the issue, people don't realize what they're saying and how it makes people feel on the other side of the conversation.

Authenticity then becomes the great equalizer. Not only does it allow you to overcome those awkward moments and bring everything to the surface, it will energize you as well.

There are other factors at play, however, when it comes to being authentic in the workplace. For example, there has been an unwritten separation of church and state in the office that you don't talk about divisive issues such as religion or politics. While it probably helps prevent arguments or uncomfortable situations, it regrettably encourages hiding who you really are.

But what if you are Catholic and show up to work on Ash Wednesday with ashes on your forehead? Should you avoid talking about religion when your religion is out there for everyone to see? Should people be discouraged to ask you about it? If your religion is a significant part of who you are, how can you authentic if you aren't allowed to mention it?

Part of authenticity is learning how to be respectful of others who hold different viewpoints than you. Why should we accept teaching people not to talk about things rather than stressing out a just a little bit and learn how to be respectful to others and, in the process, be more authentic?

Say you're a fierce Republican and I'm a fierce Democrat. We likely voted differently. Why can't we just have a cordial conversation about our differences? Why does something like this have to be off limits?

Another benefit of being authentic is that you learn what and how other people think and what they believe. You become more respectful of others because you're comfortable in your own skin. It may not always be easy, but it certainly carries with it long-lasting results.

The Enemies of Authenticity

By now you're probably saying to yourself, "But what about all the roadblocks to becoming authentic?"

Yes, the enemies are out there. There are a lot of them.

One of the biggest is being scared or fearful. But I have also seen different roadblocks and enemies based on whether the person involved was a man or a woman. Alas, gender is one of the greatest enemies of authenticity.

From an early age, women are told what we should be: we should be good girls; we shouldn't cause trouble; we should become teachers or nurses; we should do what our dads tell us to do; we need to get married and have a family. Men, on the other hand, face a large roadblock if their authentic self is not the standard norm of what a man should be—such as a male nurse or someone who is softer and more caring; who enjoys crafting instead of sports.

Another enemy is more obvious: We do not regularly talk about authenticity. It's not something we discuss, and it's not something we often enough coach our kids to embrace as they are growing up.

Sometimes, as unfortunate as it is, your partner can be the roadblock to authenticity. If your partner isn't open to change, and you're a different person today than you were five, 10, or even 15 years ago, it will hinder your ability to become who you really are.

One example of this involves one of my favorite former coworkers who is also a close friend. Her partner was assigned male at birth, but later in their marriage grew to realize and acknowledge her true gender identity as a transgender woman. My friend embraced their marriage, refusing to be a roadblock and choosing to continue to love and accept her partner's (wife's) new authentic self, as did the family they have together. They are both amazing.

For many couples in this situation the roadblocks are insurmountable. Therefore, I don't fool myself into thinking this will happen all the time, but ultimately, what it demonstrates is you will never achieve authenticity unless you recognize the need for change, face your enemy or roadblock, and muster up enough courage to act on it.

Sometimes, changing your environment is crucial. In the workplace, if you are never going to be seen or treated as more than an intern or lower-ranking person, no matter how authentic you are to yourself you must have the courage to move on. You must face that enemy and challenge yourself to overcome the roadblock—and be courageous enough to trust you'll find a better opportunity elsewhere.

Achieving Authenticity

It is important to recognize you will not just wake up one day and suddenly be authentic. Even though I've been practicing for years, I'm still practicing. Authenticity is a journey; not a destination. It is okay to be less than perfect. As long as you're learning about yourself, you can strive toward authenticity. Continuous learning is part of the process.

So, what are steps you can take toward achieving authenticity?

Invest time. Learn about yourself. Be with yourself (i.e., go to a coffee shop and read a book, take a walk in the woods/nature, do anything that connects with your inner-being).

Be willing to grow and change who you are—or who you think you are. Be comfortable making changes to yourself.

Take some time to think about the words that define you, as well as what words others would use to describe you. If they don't match up, figure out why and do something about it.

As a leader, if you're authentic, find ways to develop a culture of authenticity throughout your organization. Begin with an assessment tool that analyzes social styles, or a Myers-Briggs test. Have the team do it together, and then have a skilled facilitator talk though the results. Then, make the necessary adjustments to how you approach people based on your new understanding of who they are.

This requires a lot of energy and focus, but will yield big, positive results.

To achieve personal authenticity, pick one or two things to do and start doing these things in a safe environment (i.e., you want to be happy, an easy first step is to smile and say hi to people when you go anywhere).

Use some sort of tool to figure out what do you want in life—either over the next few months or years. Then, build a plan for how you are going to get there.

Authenticity also requires you to make yourself a priority. This is especially important for women. We do a terrible job of putting ourselves at the center of our universe. Instead, we everyone else a priority. Think of it like a sponge. A sponge won't work after you've sucked all the moisture from it. You must determine how to replenish yourself. For me, I look at it like a jar: the best way to fill a jar is to put in rocks, then pebbles, then sand, and then water. Prioritize! Put in the big things (rocks) first, which will leave room for the smaller items (pebbles, sand, water). Saying "no" to the little things you're asked to do on a daily basis can be a challenge. It may not feel authentic to say "no", and you might feel bad in the moment. But you won't be authentic to yourself if you stretch yourself thin, and end up resenting everything else you do.

Taken as a whole, there are four main pillars of authenticity: communication, self-care, courage, continuous learning.

You can't be your authentic self if you are not willing to communicate. However, you must learn how to employ the correct communication style for the environment.

Self-care is essential to authenticity. Taking care of yourself is loving yourself, which leads to you being your best authentic self when put in the most challenging situations. Self-care can mean different things to different people. The most important thing is carving out time to do what replenishes you daily, weekly, and monthly to ensure you are in a positive state of mind. Start small. Go for a 10-minute walk in the woods. Take five minutes to read in the morning. Try not to strive for perfection, rather progress.

Courage, like authenticity, is something that needs to be focused on and practiced regularly to become more natural over time. Having courage allows you to make the right choices in your life.

Melanie Greenberg, Ph.D. offers six attributes of courage in *Psychology Today* (https://www.psychologytoday.com/us/blog/the-mindful-self-express/201208/the-six-attributes-courage):

- Feeling Fear Yet Choosing to Act
- Following Your Heart
- Persevering in the Face of Adversity
- Standing Up For What Is Right
- Expanding Your Horizons; Letting Go of the Familiar

Continuous learning is critical to finding authenticity. As we age, we evolve and need to be consistently evaluating who we are and what we stand for. Reflecting weekly on what you would have approached differently is a great place to start. Taking courses to improve your areas of improvement will allow you to grow.

In general, the key is to never stop asking questions and ensure you have the data to be your best self.

Being your authentic self will not happen overnight, however it will happen in time with an intentional approach. I challenge you to do the work and see what beauty lies ahead. The workplace will create a more inclusive culture when authenticity is embraced.

Authenticity Checklist

- Did I behave the way I wanted to today?
- Did I act with courage today?
    - Emotionally honest
    - Set boundaries
    - Be vulnerable
- Did I show compassion today?
    - Connections
    - Create an environment of belonging
- Was I wholehearted today?
    - Sincere
    - Commitment
- Did I take care of myself today?
    - Kind
    - Self-care
    - Exercise
    - Emotional care
- Did I practice gratitude today?
    - Grace
    - Joy
    - Thank you
- Do I feel confident in my actions today?
    - Calm
    - At peace
    - Learning
- Am I happy?
    - Low stress
    - Smile
    - Feedback

Lee Ann Cochran

Lee Ann Cochran is a well-versed professional with expertise across the aerospace, defense, start-up and nonprofit industries. She received her B.S. in Materials Science & Engineering from The Ohio State University and has advanced her career with experience in research, development, process scaling, manufacturing, proposal development, capture management, business development, sales, marketing and licensing.

A passionate volunteer, Lee Ann spends her free time supporting causes which champion human rights and equality. Among these, she advocates to give women and girls access to education, actively participates with the United Nations Commission on the Status of Women, is dedicated to advancing the cultures of diversity and inclusion in STEM, and volunteers in the community.

Lee Ann received the Women in Engineering ProActive Network (WEPAN) Presidents award in 2018. She was recognized as a 2017 Smart Business Progressive Woman in Cleveland and in 2016 was selected for the Outstanding Soroptimist Award for Columbus and Franklin County. Lee Ann was also named as one of the 2014 Women You Should Know by Women for Economic and Leadership Development (WELD) and acknowledged by Battelle as a Women's History Month Honoree for bringing forward ideas to drive change and shape the future. Her unique background in engineering and sales allows for her to lead fundraising efforts for nonprofits in a positive way. Additionally, Lee Ann values authenticity and a purpose-driven life.

How to Build a Culture of Caring
THERESE ZDESAR

(Hint: Invest in your people—personally & professionally)

Caring is an important part of who I am and one of the many reasons why I wanted to become a nurse—to care and serve others. Originally, I thought I would be a life flight or military nurse, but my experience of working with seniors through nursing school was close to my heart. Unfortunately, seniors are often not given enough respect as our treasurers in society. So, I set out to change that.

When I was a young nurse, I saw firsthand how different the quality of life was for seniors—especially those that could remain in place aging at home. I told myself I thought I could do it better—seniors needed to stay at home with compassionate care, extraordinary quality service, and love. As fortune would have it, I ran into the concept of Home Instead Senior Care, a Nebraska-based franchisor of non-medical in-home care for the elderly.

The timing could not have been more perfect: I had just become a mom and I was seeking something to fulfill myself as a mom and a professional—and I didn't want to miss precious moments with my baby.

Entrepreneurship—becoming a franchisee of Home Instead—was my solution. It was the scariest but one of the best decisions I've ever made. And since I became an entrepreneur in 2000, one of the most important lessons I've learned as a business owner is the value of building a workplace culture. In fact, I have learned that if you leverage by deliberate design a company culture, your company will have far more opportunity than you can ever image. Business culture is the living breathing core of your business. It is the part that your employees and customers actually feel. One of my favorite quotes is by Maya Angelou: "I've learned that people will forget what you said, people will forget what you did, but people will never forget how you made them feel." Business culture is exactly that part that your customers and employees will never forget.

In 2012, my small independently owned company achieved the *Inc.* top 5000 recognition of fastest growing companies. When I was asked how we achieved this I always humbly explained it was our amazing caregivers. What I didn't understand at the time it was definitely our amazing team that made my business a success, but it was also our business culture that drove this success. I have always believed that people more than business plans or any physical assets make a strong growing business. If you want to serve your clients well—and we are all in the service business in some way—you must first start by looking inside the company at your culture. It's what makes your business unique and is the sum of its values, traditions, beliefs, interactions, behaviors, and attitudes. Your culture will attract talent, drives engagement, impacts happiness and satisfaction, and affects performance. The personality of your business is influenced by everything you place value on and for me our most important asset has always been our employees

In our company, our caregivers are primarily providing non-medical type of services, which may be anything from laundry and errands, transportation, or assistance with personal care—like bathing and dressing. Think of it like receiving all the amenities of an assisted living facility but in the comfort of one's own home.

Each month, we serve more than 300 clients. The amount of time spent with any given client varies from three hours each day to up to 24 hours each day, depending on the needs of the aging adult

Yet, for all the focus on customer service, achieving this level wasn't an overnight process. It required us to establish a strong foundation internally, and then build upon it while we tweaked what we were doing and nurtured its growth. It is, however, something any business can achieve—if management, ownership and the employees put their collective mind to it. In doing so, you can create a sustainable, scalable, and effective organization with a caring culture.

So why is a strong culture so important as the underpinning to all of this?

First and foremost, people want to work for a place where they feel that their work matters and where they feel respected. We take that a step further. We know that people perform best when they feel like they are part of a family; where they are cared about. We strive to make people feel fulfilled in their personal life and their business life.

The biggest challenge for employers today—beyond finding good, qualified employees—is keeping them by creating a culture within their business that allows and individual to feel fulfilled and part of something bigger than themselves. It's no secret that we all want human connection. We all want to feel part of a family. And this applies to both our clients and our caregivers. We want our clients to feel as if their caregivers are a part of their family; like they are being taken care of by a family member.

We believe that for our caregivers to feel like the clients are family, they need to feel like they belong to the Home Instead family. You become an extension of someone else's family when you work in their business, so if we, as business owners, don't create a culture where we treat others as an extension of our family, how can we expect our employees to do that?

It comes down to teaching by example. Walking the talk. And building a workforce of people who all believe the same thing, who are all working together as part of the same value system and are unified in striving for a similar goal. When you pick each other up, and you treat people the way you want to be treated, you're well on your way to establishing a culture of caring.

In our case, we teach our team members how to make others feel the same way they do by treating them with respect. Our hope is that they continue to carry the culture on to others, and then into our clients' homes.

So how can you build a strong business culture of caring?

1. Hire the right people

My biggest challenge in this business—as it is for most employers—is hiring and maintaining extraordinary people. I don't hire bodies. Instead, I hire people who care about delivering quality service to others. And in most cases, what we ask people to do transcends service. It becomes companionship.

The key to our early success, which allowed us to become the fastest growing franchise in the network ever, was accomplished because we were laser-focused on finding extraordinary people, training them, and then treating them with the highest level of respect.

The typical person we hired was someone around age 50—around the right age to be a daughter to the seniors we were serving—and often an early retiree because early retirees sometimes must subsidize their Social Security. Most of them are women; and several are churchgoing ladies. They are the type of people who may have taken care of a mother who passed away and find fulfillment in giving back to others. They are people who others turn to in times of need because they're natural caregivers. However, as natural caregivers, they often have their own families to tend to—which means it is hard for them to work full-time at Home Instead. This created a different problem as our greatest blessing led to our biggest curse: most of our workers aren't full-time employees. So, we have all these amazing people whom the clients love… but we can only use them part of the time.

We learned early on that the best people to hire are those who get fulfillment from being a caregiver and are not be determined to squeeze every extra cent out of an employer. Obviously, we believe in a fair wage, but the best fit for us was someone who believed in the mission first. Often, this was someone who has experienced something in their lives that left an impact—such as caring for an elderly parent. Here's an example: Our billing specialist, Luann, begged me for a job for six months after we cared for her mother. We made such an impact that she felt she absolutely needed to work with us and impact others in the same way we had with her. Luann was passionate about Home Instead. But I didn't think she was ready to be in the role. She didn't give up, and literally harassed me into giving her a position.

Luann is one of our most valuable employees. In addition to billing, she does our intake, which oftentimes means matching clients with caregivers according to what their passions are. Her role is also to connect with the family members of clients and help to explain to them what we can do for their loved one. I think it helps her still feel connected to her mother, who passed.

This is partly a sales process because it's explaining to someone what we do and how we do it, and then getting them to agree to have us come in and do a consultation. Luann probably does this better than anyone has before because of the passion she feels about what we do and who we are. But that's an example of the type of people who contribute to building a culture of caring. And because of our approach, we have a great group of fighters in our office—a group of women who truly care about each other and our mission to serve clients.

Identify the fit

I used to do personality testing before I hired individuals to identify common traits that lined up individuals with certain positions. However, we stopped doing the standard testing because we found the traits with the biggest effects are those things you can't monitor. It's love; the way that you can relate and get along with other people.

It's passion for what we're doing. It's that little internal light you see in people that makes them different. We can train someone on job skills, but you can't change the core of who someone is—and in business, who someone is at their core is often one of the most important traits to consider in a potential hire.

Competition also makes it harder to find good people—and depending on your industry, it can create a real challenge. When we were starting out, we used to be one of the only ones who provided this type of service. Today, there are several retirement communities which offer similar services, as well as other companies that open each year as the aging population has made this an attractive client base and target market. So, we're competing with other organizations for talent—some of whom base their decisions on where to work solely on compensation. When it becomes a battle based on compensation, few organizations in any industry can win if they are just bidding up the salary and benefits. That's why it's so important to find people who want to do the type of work your organization does for the right reason.

For us, if the choice is between keeping a loving and caring culture where the clients know they are the No. 1 priority and simply expanding for expansion sake, it's no choice at all—we want to maintain a culture of caring.

Identifying those people continues to get harder. We get both types of applicants: those who apply for fulfillment and those for apply for compensation. When that happens, it is important to find ways during the interview process that allow you to effectively measure an applicant's intent, values, and passions. Sometimes, that comes through in the questions you ask. Other times, you can just sense it in how passionate a candidate is when they're talking about caring for others. It's a constant work-in-progress, but if you commit yourself to doing it, you can continuously improve.

Another challenge is that because many of the people who fit well for us can't work full-time, we are consistently updating our employees' availability. People are very concerned about their work-life balance, and people who make a good fit for us seemingly are decreasing their availability rather than increasing it. So, we find ourselves in a Catch-22 situation: How can we get enough people who are motivated out of the true desire to be care-takers but have limited hours they want to work to fill the demand? And, how can we ensure the same level of quality caregivers as we did when the demand was lower?

We have tried to address this through a bonus program within our system where individuals who work 35 hours or more each week and meet other certain criteria receive a bonus each year. It's a financial incentive for people who we've already determined that financial incentives aren't the reason they are here in the first place. For us, at least, it's the difference of using money as an incentive to work versus using money as an incentive to work more hours.

Go where the candidates are

It used to be that you could find good candidates by advertising in print. But today, it's moved online. Word of mouth is also effective, but with the type of person we're looking for, we needed to think differently about how and where to find prospective candidates. It's not an uncommon dilemma for any business owner in a niche industry.

One way we approached this was by going out into the community and looking for opportunities to talk about Home Instead. This may be an AARP group; it may be a church group; it may even be at a teachers' union meeting. Teachers' unions can be a great place to recruit because teachers have time off during the summers where they may be able to work part-time. Teachers and caregivers have very similar characteristics.

When our recruiter goes to these meetings, she creates an exciting awareness about what Home Instead is, what the culture is, and why being a caregiver is such a rewarding opportunity. When you have an opportunity to sell what you do to others face-to-face, it's a powerful recruitment tool.

Assess

Once individuals who fit our criteria are brought here, they go through a screening process that includes an interview. We need to make sure they're bondable and insured. They also go through a background check. Beyond that, we want candidates to really learn and understand what the role they're applying for is and what their experience will be at Home Instead.

One of the tools that's been put together on a more macro level is a talent assessment page. When people fill out applications online, they fill out the talent assessment page. While it's a good tool, it impersonalizes some of the process. The qualities I look for in a candidate are difficult to assess through an online application. You need a giving heart to fill the type of positions we have. This means we ask questions that aren't typical interview questions—going beyond the talent assessment tool. Every employer should consider adding a layer like this to ensure people who have the necessary skills to do the job also have the requisite passion and nature to be part of the corporate culture you've established at your company and want to continue to nurture.

In home care, we are involved in a type of work that can negatively affect someone if they're heart isn't in the job. We work with people who need help. It can include long, grueling, and odd hours. For those people who see it as "work" rather than a calling, the effect of caring for people who can't care for themselves can turn negative quickly and then have a direct impact on a vulnerable person's quality of life. On average, we hire one out of every ten applicants that come to our offices.

Some of the questions we end up asking to probe people and learn more about their energy level, frustration tolerance, service attitude, dependability, and empathy include:

- What time of the work day are you at your peak performance?
- Tell me about a time you had to work at a fast pace for an extended period of time. How did you maintain your work pace?
- Tell me about a time when you became frustrated at work. What were the circumstances? What did you do? How did the situation get resolved?
- Tell me about a time when the client wasn't sure what they needed, and you helped to identify this.
- Tell me about a time when you were able to understand how someone else was feeling even though they weren't stating it to you. How did you take appropriate action?
- Describe a time when you had to change your approach to a client because your initial attempts were unsuccessful.
- Give me an example of a time when you experience an emotionally upset person. How did you deal with him or her?
- Tell me about a decision you made at work where you had to disregard your own personal feelings. What was your role in the situation, and how did it work out?
- Give me an example of something you have done in your previous job that demonstrated how others can depend on you.

The importance of ethics & trust

One of the most important guiding principles for any culture of caring is ethics. It must permeate everything you do. In our case, not only are we held to state and federal standards, but we have developed our own standards.

Ethics—and the morals that guide an organization—start at the top. The owner or leader of a company must set the standard for others to follow. And then must hold their leadership team and the administrative team to those ethical standards. They, in turn, hold everyone else to those standards, which in our case means the caregivers.

One example we faced was when one of the general managers called me to let me know a client's family claimed a ring was missing from the senior's home.

That's a very real dilemma. We have 300 caregivers and 300 clients. No matter how diligent you are with background checks, things happen. It's important to teach your staff—hopefully, by example—how to handle this type of situation with transparency and care.

We responded immediately, which included calling the police. We also sent out a case manager to investigate.

As it turned out, the woman simply lost the ring in her house and found it a week later. But how we handled the situation—and our immediate and serious response—underscores the importance of ethics within our culture of caring.

2. Invest in your people

You invest in people the moment you make a hire. And it never really stops once they come on board.

Our Human Resources department conducts the official onboarding and orientation for our company, and part of their role is to continue building excitement about becoming part of Home Instead Senior Care.

Every week, we have training classes for new team members. Orientation training takes two days. On day one, the new employee's name is placed on a whiteboard. Staff comes in, meets them, greets them with excitement, and introduces them to Home Instead. The general manager comes in and does the same. If I am here, I make sure to spend time with the orientation training class. We make sure it is a fun, positive, and happy experience.

On the first day, new hires review the employee handbook, company policy, how to document work, ethics and expectations. And, most important, we discuss our culture of caring.

The second day is geared toward hands-on, practical application for care of seniors. This may include bathing, dressing, and other clinical parts of the work we do. Most people leave the initial training with a direct job placement; something that immediately connects them to us.

And, as I mentioned, training doesn't end once orientation has ended. When you invest in your people, this includes providing continuous training, improvement opportunities, and just as important, treating people with the respect they deserve. Beyond fair wages, we show respect through other intrinsic values such as gratitude, appreciation, and development opportunities. If you want to foster a culture of caring once you've developed it, you absolutely need to invest in your people.

Provide continuous training

When you provide continuous training, it should include more than just keeping people up to date on the latest and greatest techniques. It must incorporate helping your employees learn how to do better within the existing job they have. We call it the career journey, and when you help people continuously improve upon what they're currently doing, it opens new opportunities for growth beyond their existing role.

Close to 80 percent of our administrative team is comprised of people who started as caregivers and rose through the ranks in our organization. We've also seen caregivers move on to higher-level positions at other Home Instead franchises across the country.

We let every employee know the opportunity for upward growth exists, but it is up to them to communicate with us what their needs are. I never want our caregivers to feel like they must work administratively in the office to have an upward step in their career path because everyone is on their own journey. Some caregivers may not feel at all fulfilled by answering the phone and taking a client's inquiry. But someone may very well need that job at some point because of physical limitations or because they're a little burnt out from caregiving and still want to be in contact with people to feel as though they're making a difference.

Create upward opportunities

We have never advertised for an administrative position. Applicants came to us either because we hand-picked them when they were serving as a caregiver or our because our caregivers knew about different opportunities and were comfortable enough to approach us about them.

This holds true with nearly any company in any industry—when you look inside your organization, you will likely find exactly what you're looking for among the team members who have done good work and shown their commitment to—and passion for—your company.

Our two general managers demonstrated excellent leadership skills and proved themselves in other administrative roles prior to becoming general managers. The caregivers who we put "on call" are ones who have exhibited leadership and caring skills that enable them to communicate in an effective way with others. We make sure there is always someone answering the phones rather than a service or machine; so, it's important to have people in our office who can speak with clients or potential clients, help them, and make them feel well cared for—no matter what time of day or night it is.

When we interview and hire applicants, especially administratively, I ask them what their five-year plan looks like, as well as where and how they want to grow. This gives them an opportunity to share their thoughts, and for me to learn a little more about what they want their future to look like. And, in my experience, the employees who shone the brightest in their caregiver roles were the ones who fell into administrative roles and found great success there. When positions open, we evaluate existing employees before we even think about reaching out to someone outside the company.

Develop specialized training opportunities

We take the training of our new caregivers very seriously; it's a higher intensity and level of training than many of our competitors. We have internal certifications. We have a hospice certification. And we have an Alzheimer's certification. We also secured a Veteran's Administration contract, so we're added that as well.

The VA contract is an example of a specialized training opportunity that grew out of one of our employees' passions. Luann, who had stalked me for six months before we hired her, asked me if she could pursue this. There are a lot of veterans within our client population, so it made sense to us. It's also underscores how important listening to employees is and why passionate people can be one of the best assets any company has. Specialized training allows people who have a passion in a specific area to feel fulfilled and for you to expand your company's service offerings.

I tasked Luanne with writing a VA training once we landed the contract. There are numerous things you need to do differently with veterans that you don't need to do with other groups. One such difference involved being aware of—and prepared for—post-traumatic stress disorder (PTSD). Veterans that suffer from PTSD have different needs. For example, you should never approach a veteran from the rear. We've seen injuries caused by the knee-jerk reactions to someone coming up on a veteran from behind. In another case, we had a client who wouldn't take a bath. It required us telling him he needed to be ready by 0800 hours because the Sergeant needed to see him bathed and dressed. Once we put it in terms he could understand, he was able to do what he previously could not.

It's this type of specialized training—and ensuring you develop opportunities for your team members to pursue them—that can enhance an already-strong culture of caring.

Make onboarding critical

Many organizations view onboarding as a necessary component but don't always see the value in ensuring people complete it with the same level of passion as they had when they joined the organization. If you simply get people on board, then move to the next group, you do a disservice to your team. Instead, when you make onboarding a critical part of the process, you'll build instant loyalty and add another strong member to the team.

For the first 30 days of any new employee's tenure with Home Instead, new caregivers are guided and nurtured by existing caregivers to ensure they're not drowning in their role. I call it putting them in a little baby incubator.

Our HR department has been tasked with maintaining a turnover level at lower than 40 percent. This means their role is to ensure every new employee's experience is positive, and that they have the training, support, and encouragement to stay with us for an extended time. Experience has shown us that turnover usually occurs during that early period, so we're focused on developing and implementing effective ways to ensure a good retention rate.

For example, after a new caregiver's first shift with a client, they receive a call to see how the experience went. We ask probing questions, such as:
• Do you have concerns?
• Were you scared?
• What was a positive?
• What was a negative?
• What can we do to continue to encourage and support you?

And then, we end the call by telling the caregiver we are always there for them, at any time, for any need.

Cross-train across the organization

People feel valued when you invest in expanding their skill set. An easy way to do this is to expose and educate them about the roles of others across your organization.

A Home Instead caregiver never goes to a client's home without a formal administrative staff introduction and training on what that role involves. We also have more than one person informed about our clients and their respective needs. By doing so, if there is a call-off because a caregiver is sick, or their child is sick, or whatever the situation, we can turn to our existing staff or assign a different caregiver to the case without missing a beat.

Instead of cold-calling a caregiver and saying, "This is where Mrs. Smith lives and this is what she needs today. Can you go take her to the grocery store and then take her to a doctor's appointment?" we are able to send them out educated about the client. In those cases, the situation might involve providing the new caregiver with every piece of information we have on Mrs. Smith, then taking her to Mrs. Smith's home. And then, conversation might go like this: "Mrs. Smith, I am your case manager, Jennifer and I would like to introduce you to your caregiver Sarah. We have trained Sarah on your care plan and what have told us is important to you. She is going to be your caregiver today while your regular caregiver is sick. Is there anything special you would like me to show Sarah or make sure she knows about what you would like today?"

We usually rely on our case manager to handle this role because case managers know the clients well and have built relationships. There is also often a direct shadowing process for new caregivers where they follow an existing caregiver for a certain period. The nurses will go out with them initially, introduce the caregiver to the client, and together review the plan of care. We usually do this when we know someone is going to be taking a vacation and needs someone to fill in for her while she's gone.

This type of cross-training process ensures we alleviate the senior's fear of having a stranger in their home to take care of them. It serves two purposes: the seniors are in a very vulnerable population; and our caregivers feel completely comfortable in their role and with their client. Our goal is to make introductions and that no person is ever blindly sent to a senior's home. The caregivers consistently tell us this process enhances their experience.

3. Create a family atmosphere

We create an environment where our employees feel part of the family. This includes making an investment in them as people, not just as employees. We build relationships with them; we know their grandchildren's names; we know them as human beings. We recognize it is more than a business and our employees are an extension of our family. This is one of the most important parts of the caring culture of my business. I introduce myself to every new employee personally and with a phone call and welcome them to the family. I explain to each employee that we are truly there for them throughout their caregiving journey to support them and they are never alone when in the field. I know that by modeling this important value and treating my caregivers as family they in turn will remember to treat the seniors they care for as family! I also model this value for my staff in how we treat everyone in our business with the same respect we would treat our family.

Many business owners claim to create a family atmosphere for their employees. But, fostering a culture where everyone feels the same way is much harder to accomplish—and requires constant attention. It must be part of your core values and spoken about and modeled consistently.

Build relationships

We had an employee on our team named Lucy. One moment, Lucy and I would have a conversation about filling a case. Then, for the next 15 minutes we would talk about her brother, who at the time was sick. And so, over time, our relationship was built. Lucy felt like she was a member of the family, and we felt the same way. Realistically, a business owner cannot always spend that much time nurturing every person in his or her company, but if you want to create a family atmosphere you have to spend enough time building relationships that make it work.

As a new business owner, I found myself building relationships during normal business hours, when I could talk to people, and doing business-related tasks at night. I would spend time working on billing late at night, toiling until the early hours of the morning. But during the day, I would build relationships with as many people as I could. Now as an established business of almost 20 years, I hold this same critical value and our administrative team builds relationships with depth in all touch points of our business.

The benefits of building relationships can be exponential. One example is when a member of my administrative team took over custody caring for her grandson as her daughter went through recovery treatments. She was extremely stressed out over the situation. My general manager saw something was going on with her personal life that was causing her distress and approached her about it. Because the general manager had taken the time to build a relationship with her team member, the woman opened up about what was going on. Once the general manager learned about the situation, and how she was taking care of her grandson because she could not afford to anything about it, she reached out to me.

That's when we stepped in as extended members of her family. We sponsored her grandson to attend a special camp for the summer. It was perhaps a $500 investment for us, but it was an investment in her. She saw we cared about her, and it made a difference in her life. That's what family does. These investments are always given with the knowledge that they're not ever going to have to pay this back. We let them know, "This is for you because we care about you, and we value you and your family, and we value everything that you do."

Make it fun

When people go through orientation training, we make it fun and informative making sure we provide a special lunch with the administrative team. We also have a short graduation good bye where the team presents the new employee with a rose and "clap out". We want that initial experience with our company to leave a strong feeling of our culture of caring. We stress that anything we can do to make their experience with us enjoyable and great is what is most important to us. My message is always: "We just want you to feel not only as if you are part of our family, but to treat others like your family. Our door is always open here."

Once people are on board, there are other initiatives under way to keep the fun going. One is the quarterly cook out meeting, which is always amusing and fun. The people in HR have funny personalities. They'll plan games and entertainment that gets the crowd engaged. When you do the type of work we do, where emotions can run deep, finding ways to balance that with fun is important.

Another fun initiative is part of our annual Christmas celebration. We create a song-and-dance number for our caregivers, which is always a hit. They like it because the administrative team is making fun of themselves, being ridiculous, and having a good time. It doesn't have to be much. Sometimes, it is just those little things that allow people to step away from reality for a moment or two to enjoy themselves or do something crazy that makes people feel part of one big family.

Care for one another

What's the one thing every family does, no matter what the relationships within it look like? Take care of one another. We are no different. We take the responsibility for the wellness and quality of life of our caregivers very seriously. How can we expect them to take care of their seniors if we don't take care of them?

Here's an example: We had a caregiver who was in a horrible automobile accident and suffered traumatic brain injury. She was not supposed to live. It took this poor young lady almost three years to be functional again. When she was finally able to function, she came back to us and said, "I know I can't do a whole lot, I know my memory has been impaired, but I need to do something. Do you have something for me?"

We put her to work filing for about three hours per week. Not everything was accurate all the time, but we didn't mind. Our welcoming her back and finding a place for her in the organization fulfilled her. We did this because she was part of our family. The difference it made in her life was significant. But then again, that's what family does—care for each other when they need it most. Modeling this value for my staff continued to infuse my business with the culture of caring.

Know your people's strengths and best fits

When you take the time in any organization to match people with their personalities and traits, it allows them to feel fulfilled in the role they're in. In addition to choosing their hours, we allow our caregivers to match with clients that they strongly bond with. Some people find value in taking care of hospice clients; others prefer taking care of those with Alzheimer's. Caregivers choose which clients are good match for them, and that is one of the guarantees we've always given our families and our caregivers: you will be matched with the right person.

We profile each of our caregivers when they first come in, and so we know most things about them: Do you play the piano? Do you speak a second language? What are your interests? Religion is always very important to our seniors. By helping match some of those things, we can be assured of a better chance for a good relationship to evolve between client and caregiver.

Not all things can be determined on paper, however, so that's where the love and dedication of our caregivers come in. One of our clients was Mrs. P. She had lost her husband and wanted companionship. I matched a caregiver with her—an older woman who was around 60 years old and not much younger than Mrs. P. They were an amazing fit. They both had quirky, funny personalities, and we would get calls from them where they would be laughing and having a good time.

But then, something happened.

Before he passed, Mr. P would play the organ for Mrs. P every night. It was their thing. Once she learned about this, Mrs. P's caregiver soon began to harass me, saying, "I can't continue with Mrs. P, I need someone who can play the organ."

This was in the early days of our business, so I replied, "I only have 20 caregivers on staff. I'll do my best."

Finally, after we went back and forth several times and I hadn't yet found anyone, the caregiver called me and said, "Just forget it."

I was confused. "I'm sorry," I said. "I thought you wanted me to replace you. Why the change of heart?"

She replied, "I took piano lessons."

This is the type of people we hire, and the commitment people make when they feel like they want to ensure a great fit. She took piano lessons! Well, it wasn't long before we received another call—we were invited to a concert at Mrs. P's house.

When we arrived, they played "Twinkle, Twinkle Little Star," and they were laughing like it was the greatest thing in the world. That was how she connected she had become with Mrs. P.

Our caregivers naturally find ways to make these connections, but we've developed other ways to offer tips and advice through our experiences. We have even created a list of one hundred ways you can connect with a human being. It's so important in this business to connect on that human level—which makes our efforts to match people that much more critical. While we look for little things, like funny personality traits or a love of food, it really becomes those little things that are most effective in establishing genuine human connections.

Maintaining the right culture and environment is something that we really work hard on. Our workplace isn't just an office—it's an extended home for everyone involved. We are all part of one giant family, and we want our culture of caring to spread through every home we are invited into and he lives of every person we touch: employees, clients, and family members. This mentality starts when people have their first interaction with us and continues every single day.

4. Listen

When you're building a culture of caring, you won't know what works and what doesn't unless you engage team members. That means listening, and really listening to what people say. It requires soliciting input, and then doing something concrete with it. If you're simply asking people for their thoughts to make them feel good without following through, your team members will see those gestures for what they are—empty. Instead, strong cultures listen to employees and find ways to take their feedback and improve the entire organization.

Ask for feedback—the good, the bad, and the ugly

Our parent company does a good job in their attempts to measure satisfaction. They partner with J.D. Power to survey clients and caregivers, providing us with feedback in near-real-time.

We take those results and go one step further: we use it to assemble town hall meetings with our caregivers and discuss what's on their mind. Over the years, we have made adjustments and changes based upon their feedback and these meetings.

What has been even more powerful are a series of focus groups, comprised of caregivers, that we hold each quarter. During the focus groups, we again solicit feedback, such as asking what changes we can make or what is it the caregivers are looking for from us. We then can determine what we are doing well, and what areas we need to address for change or improvement.

While we hear about many traditional things—pay, hours, etc.— what we're really seeking are things we do right and things we need to improve: Do you feel appreciated? Do you feel valued? Do you feel rewarded? Can we retain you? These are specific questions that elicit specific answers where we can act. The focus groups are powerful because it's a two-way communication vehicle—they offer feedback, we respond, and they see us act on the feedback.

Our bereavement group was originally a suggestion from one of our focus groups. One of our caregivers told us she was struggling with the loss of two clients that were like family to her. "Why don't you guys do something?" she asked.

So, we took the idea and created a grievance ceremony.

Our hospice partners offer to provide their ministers or spiritual consults to us whenever we need them. Our bereavement ceremonies go like this: We have candles at each table and flowers throughout the entire meeting place. We put up a little plaque with all the clients' names that have passed within that quarter. When everyone is present, we do a non-denominational prayer, and the caregivers who has served one of those clients brings up a candle and has the opportunity to share stories about their senior.

In addition to this ceremony, caregivers who recently lost a senior goes through an assessment, so we can determine if they need to have any additional bereavement counseling. If they do need additionally counseling, we provide it. This entire concept came out of one of our focus groups.

Another example of listening to our employees involves the creation of our vision statement. It is one of the most important parts of our company, and it was a staff-led initiative.

As a franchisee of Home Instead, we have a corporate mission statement, which is "To enhance the lives of aging adults and their families." It's on our wall and there to remind us as our guiding principle as an organization. But it didn't necessarily represent our culture, which was pointed out to us by our team members. And so, together we worked hard and developed our vision statement: "To lead and serve with trusted expertise from the heart."

What I like about our one-sentence vision statement is that it is something referable and relevant. When a problem arises, you can quickly go back and see if how you address it follows our collective vision. It helps individuals to take a step back and see the real reason we exist. It defines who we are and demonstrates how much we value each other.

Our vision statement was created collectively by employees during one of our annual administrative staff retreats. Once it was determined we would develop one, everyone knew how important it would be. They began brainstorming words that included what they wanted to be, or which described us as a team or our values.

After developing a list of words, the staff started voting on each of them and eliminating word after word from the list. There were approximately 50 words on the initial list, and as they voted and eliminated, they kept getting closer and closer to landing on exactly what they believed were our guiding values—as well as what was the most important way of expressing it.

With a narrowed down list, they began creating different versions of what would eventually become our vision statement. And finally, they agreed on the one that graces our office walls today. When it was done, everyone read it aloud and said, "Wow, that really describes everything that we want it to describe about us."

This statement conveys what's most important to all of us: We want to be the expert in senior care; a leader. Service was important, and we talk a lot about what it means to be a servant leader. Culture was important...a.k.a. the heart and being a family. These were the guiding principles most important to the staff, so these were the ideas that made it into the statement.

I think these are very powerful words and they lead to the only question we need to ask ourselves about an action or a choice we need to make. I've used our vision statement to reel an employee back in when they start to feel negative about something. It becomes easy to say, "Go back to the vision. Is this coming from your heart? Are you leading with compassion? Are you being a leader? Or are you being a follower in the situation? Would a leader make those choices?"

What's more, it's easy to remember because it's one sentence. And that was the point! If we had to describe Home Instead or what it is we do, this is the alternative to saying, "We're a non-medical company who provides care in the home."

Instead, it sums it up beautifully. This is what we do. This is our culture. This is what we believe in. And we wouldn't have developed it had we not taken the time to listen to our team.

5. Communicate and Celebrate

Even the best culture can't survive on caring alone. That's why it's important to establish vehicles where you can communicate to all team members, as well as take the time to celebrate.

Our monthly training sessions and caregiver meetings are great opportunities to fill everybody up and then send them back out. But we knew we needed more ways to connect on a regular basis. So, we developed monthly newsletters that help keep our culture thriving.

These newsletters are an opportunity to not only communicate what is going on in the company, but also a way to make the company feel more like a family—especially because we don't all work in the same place. Through the newsletter we share recipes, celebrate people's birthdays and work anniversaries, and give shout-outs to people who have been extraordinary.

Examples of items include:

• Caregiver of the month
• Details around how a newly implemented scheduling method benefited team members, along with information on how to access it and set up an account to get started
• Reminders on dress codes and paperwork
• How to maintain a "can-do" attitude when the going gets rough
• Upcoming events, including volunteerism opportunities

There are numerous other ways to celebrate. Beyond the newsletter, everybody in our company receives something from administration on their birthday and anniversary—more than just the newsletter shout-out. We mail something to their home—usually a signed card from everyone in the administrative office on birthdays and anniversaries, along with a small gift card.

Sometimes, the best ideas for celebrating comes from a negative experience. I was sitting in a meeting one day, listening to the administrative team. There was a lot of focus on one complaint, and it was receiving every ounce of attention.

Finally, I knew we had to stop this behavior and eliminate the negativity which was permeating the meeting. Is said, "OK, we're going to measure this. And we're going to start a compliment/complaint program."

I showed the staff how they could measure every interaction they had with a client. These interactions, I explained, were an opportunity to truly hear what someone was saying—are they complaining or are they happy?

Our plan was to document the complaints and the compliments. We would measure for one full week and analyze the results. I told them, "I bet you're going to have a 10:1 ratio; 10 people very happy against one complaint."

When the results came in, I was correct. We read them aloud as a group and realized we'd done some really great things that week. After some discussion, we decided to share them with the caregivers, so we could let them know what an awesome job they were doing, as well as the positive impact they were having on people's lives.

While this program became an opportunity to promote our positives and hear the good things, we didn't ignore the one negative comment. Instead, we learned from that negative and then focused on celebrating our growth by addressing the mistake. We all came to the realization that it was OK to make a mistake; it's what makes us human. But, if we spent too much time focused on the one bad thing, we would miss the 10 good things we had done.

Today, five years after implementing this program, we take the 10 compliments and communicate them to the team. We celebrate them together, and use sharing them as gratitude opportunities. Our HR department doles out the gratitude, and caregivers who have been complimented get handwritten notes of specific gratitude, and then receive a bonus buck. Bonus bucks are little dollars we created which can be used for cash or merchandise within our organization. Caregivers can purchase different goods they need, such as gas cards, grocery cards, and other things that are meaningful to them.

For doing something phenomenal, they receive a five-dollar bonus buck and a handwritten note saying, "Hey, Mrs. Smith told us you did something absolutely exceptional. She looks forward to every visit with you, and she couldn't imagine a better caregiver than you."

This has made a huge difference within our organization, and it has been more than simply the bonus bucks. Our team member appreciate the cards because those make them feel good about the organization and the work they're doing. It's contagious. And it's a very powerful and measurable tool.

When you're able to look at your organization from a more holistic viewpoint, you'll find that creating a culture of caring isn't rocket science. Rather, it's the product of valuing the people who work with you and creating a workplace where they want to show up every day. Like anything else, it requires nurturing, attention, and a dedication to making it thrive. And, like any good organization, if you construct a solid base and fill it with good people, great things can come from it.

Conclusion: A culture of caring

Business owners often take a passive approach to culture. They maybe figure it's not something they can control or that they even need to control. If they leave it alone, it'll all work itself out. But leaving culture to chance does more harm than good for your organization.

Culture has always been important in business. But today, it's becoming more than just a simple boardroom "buzzword". The culture in my business has become an important differentiator to set my company apart from the competition. It's also what has helped me attract and retain the loyalty of the best employees and clients.

I have seen how a culture of caring is more important than ever as people want to be part of companies that share their same values. They want to feel like their work has a purpose and makes a difference. It is truly necessary today in business to deliberately build a culture in that lives and breathes your company's values.

Therese Zdesar

Therese Zdesar, RN, BSN, is the president and owner of QualCare, LLC, dba Home Instead Senior Care. She is a graduate of the University of Akron College of Nursing; and before becoming an entrepreneur worked in both administration and as an RN in The MetroHealth System in Cleveland, Ohio. She has a deep passion and love for serving seniors, and credits her experience living with and caring for her grandmother as the heart of her beliefs.

In 2001, Therese opened QualCare, a Northeast Ohio based home care company that assists older adults with private duty care at home. Over the past two decades, she and QualCare have been the recipients of more than 50 professional and business awards, including being named by *Inc.* magazine to its prestigious *Inc.* 5000 list of fastest growing companies in America. She was named a top 10 Women Business Owner of Northeast Ohio and her business has been recognized for strong organizational culture and community philanthropic involvement.

Therese is passionate about being a servant leader and is on several boards including The United Way, The Children's Museum of Cleveland and the Chagrin Athletic Association. Therese and her husband Joe, a captain on the Cleveland Fire Department, live in Chagrin Falls, Ohio, and are the proud parents of five children. She is an active speaker on issues such as senior care, successful aging, leadership and organizational culture.